the lifecurrency

from breaking to becoming
by nivedita lakhera

what holds you back, does not exist

when you discover
that no one is coming to rescue you
when you accept
that no one is coming to rescue you
when you finally decide
that you are going to move forward by yourself
when you finally decide
that you are going to take that first step
with or without someone
that's when a massive army that always lived inside of you awakens
that's when you learn to command the power within
that waited all along for you to unleash it
that's when you begin
towards the path of several struggles, failures with or without victory
but still, you begin
but still, you dare
that's when you leave the elegance of a safe life behind
that made sense to everyone except you
and you enter in the war zone of not knowing, rugged and at times cruel
but you do that
because staying on the side you are staying is killing your soul
so, you risk the ocean that burns harsher
than the sun that's nourishing you right now
you swim through it at the risk of losing it all
for you must reach the other side
you do that without even knowing what creatures, storms,
monsters and animals live there
but you begin that journey towards the unknown
leaving what is known
because you must
because
the wait is over

written by nivedita lakhera
illustrations by nivedita lakhera

book cover by nivedita lakhera
photographs by stephanie timmons and joyan sanctis

published in the USA, first printing- 2021

attention: schools, universities, libraries, and businesses
the book is available at quantity discounts with bulk
purchases for education, business, or sales promotional use.

niveditalakhera.com

we are the heroes
we are waiting for

a half-moon is not a failure
a full moon is not a victory

phases in life are not an exception but are the rule
expect all phases and not refuse them

because the world only worships what is full and shiny
does not mean other parts of life should not be honored

love yourself in all your phases even if no one else will,
especially if no one else will
celebrate yourself in all your phases, even if no one else will,
especially if no one else will

an eclipse is a phase, not an ending

most pain is invisible
hiding behind anger and
rusting as bitterness
instead of blooming
as love and compassion

churning pain into
compassion takes time
and a lot of efforts
be patient
no one reached
there
in a day
or at times even
in one lifetime

but that's where you need to
be walking towards
from pain to compassion
and keep walking,

you will fall, you will fail
but you get up and start walking again
towards your healing,
towards the person, you deserve to be

anger is not the absence of love
it's the absence of healing

you can begin doing the right thing
even when you are wrong
especially when you are wrong

you can choose to take one step forward
even when you cannot see ahead
especially when you cannot see ahead
you can start believing in your dreams
even when no one else does
especially when no one else does
you can start walking on truth
even when all you have ever known are lies
especially when all you have ever known are lies

you can start forgiving the person who hurt you
even when you have never forgiven before
especially when you have never forgiven before
and you can begin to love yourself with full commitment
even when you have never valued
and shown commitment to yourself before
especially when you have never valued and
shown commitment to yourself before

you can begin any time
even when it's the fourth, fifth, sixth or
tenth time trying all of this or any of this
you can begin

your past doesn't predict your future
your present does, your actions do

the mind should be a beautiful place
to come home to

life is not an afterthought

it's happening right now
also, it's not going on autopilot
but it's walking on your decisions

including your decision of not making one for yourself
including making yourself numb
including you convincing yourself, this is all there is
including you telling yourself, you are helpless
including you telling yourself that
a known misery is more comfortable than the unknown one

all those lies are still a decision you are making
that is the power you have
your decisions can empower you or disempower you
they all still start with you

try the truth, try being ok with discomfort
try ok with breaking than the staying same
try movement, try being ok with falling
try eating your fears for breakfast
try thoughts that take you where you were born to go

whether you think you can or you cannot
you are going to be right
what kind of right you want
when you have limited life currency to spend

break ego to break free

it was not designed to get what you want
-the life-
that's not why it was given to you
it was given to you to become what you need to be
and at times you need to unbecome first
but since the journey must happen
towards something
it is mostly towards what you think you want
and it's ok

there is nothing wrong with that too
but know even what you think has so many limitations
even what you want has so many limitations
and it's ok for you not to know them
but it will be a good start to understand
there is a limitation

limitations that come from what you were told to want
you were conditioned to desire
you were not manufactured a few years ago
you are a child of the billion-year-old stardust
that was born before time was born
so, allow yourself little pleasures
so, allow yourself little victories
so, allow yourself little falls

and above all allow yourself to rise above all this
rise, so you can be light enough
to float above all the worldly understanding and
see how magnificently everything is designed
in your favor to become

....so, when you fall it's in your favor
when you fail it's in your favor
when you win it's in your favor
whether you want it or not, life will take its course

you don't have to figure all this right away
or even in this lifetime
till the final understanding is reached
you will be born multiple times
some falls are raising you up
some failures will become your greatest victory
understand the limitations of your limitations

and free yourself towards the wisdom of the journey

not what you get, but what you become
it was not about conquering something
but towards becoming someone you were born to become

trust me my love, and trust the universe
it's in your favor even when nothing seems favorable

so, think about what you need to become, who you need to become
the world will manifest when you walk towards it,
the world that is your one true kingdom
remember
even the greatest setbacks are taking you forward
if you allow yourself the movement
even when it doesn't feel like it

hang in there,
there is a space beyond your pain,
and it will find you- i promise

the mind is so powerful that your darkness
at times is not the absence of light
but lack of acceptance of light

stories become belief
and beliefs become our truth
and our truth becomes our children's truth
and subsequently of an entire generation's truth
and this happens when we lose the capacity or intent
to raise questions and be curious and be aware
about how consequential this all can be
our prejudice is nothing, but the stories told and fed to us
till they become a truth which is full of lies
inside our very bones of existence

the world is walking on such stories told a long time ago
and fighting each other for the past
that was not of their doing
never stopping and pausing to realize
they can start writing new stories
for themselves and future generations
anytime, any day
the better stories the more humane stories
the stories that will become reality
that is more needed than what is taught in books
that have burnt bridges
between hearts that always belonged

never stopping for knowing this simple truth
that we need each other more than before
and we can all begin accepting this any day
and start writing new stories
the stories so powerful that can set us free
from the prison of prejudice that is old stories

make new stories to make a new world,
stories that heal, not the ones that keep the trauma alive

in your brokenness
lies your wholesomeness

i don't know who needs to hear this

but last year was not normal
your mind, body, soul, and all the senses
have gone through a disaster
with no end in sight

some of you lost your friends
some of you lost your role models
some of you lost hope
some of you lost faith in your fellow citizens
to do the right things to protect you,
some of you lost joy and happiness,
some of you lost the reason to move from one day to another

some of you lost support from the people
who should have supported you
some of you lost communities and colleagues
some of you lost your physical and mental health
and some of you lost the sight ahead

none of that has happened
in recent history on such a massive and intense scale
that, all of that, was a lot to go through....

.... allow yourself that it was ok
that you did not behave correctly,
knowingly, soberly, sensibly, patiently, kindly
all through that
and then forgive yourself
which is hard to do
and then forgive others
which is harder to do

because we cannot move forward without
that basic reset button of our soul
so, mourn and grieve the death of what was
allow yourself pace and space
and stay for a while in your rock bottom

be numb, be sad, be human
that's all ok, but then you must begin
you don't begin thinking about the ending
you begin because what seems
as an end to all- is where you were born to start
you begin because you must
and you do not know otherwise
you begin without the condition of arrival
but for the compulsion of the movement...

.... you begin because you see decay in not doing so
you begin even though
no one can see the path that in your bones and flesh
like a clear vision that must manifest

you begin
with a lot of kindness towards self and others
with a quarter of hope, with leftover light
with nothing perfect

with a handful of rights in the ocean of all wrong
with a back that bleeds, with feet that burn
with eyes still full, with the mind that hurts
with a heart that's heavy

you   move   forward

because what lies on the other side is
the parts of you in waiting to join you

to meet those softer, kinder, and stronger parts of you.
for that you move forward

no, there is no path
that does not yield you something
the purpose that you seek
the purpose that is yours
doesn't reveal itself to you
as a single vectorial entity,
it's not supposed to be
a simple mathematical equation
because you are not
a simple mathematical equation
it is supposed to meet you in patches
it is supposed to enter you at times as breaking
at times through relationships
at times through trauma
at times through sudden events
at times through travel
at times through births and deaths

all of that
is never a series of comfortable events
because you are not a log of dead wood
you are an alive breathing forest
which must live all its seasons
those that are alive
cannot have wishes of the dead beings
because even in coffins
the flesh yields to change
so, while you are still above the land
you must allow yourself to move
through one phase to another
trusting each phase as the part of your story not against it
embrace it all to become all of it

don't let your fear of breaking
keep you
from your fate of becoming

in the end,
you realize that the most
beautiful parts of your life
sprout out from your
brokenness
the cracks are where
the art blooms
the curves are where
the view is majestic-
the shivering land is where
the dance of life happens

in the end, you realize
that being wholesome is about
not resisting
your breaking and
unbecoming
but making space for
manifesting, unearthing, and
taking it all in

in the end,
you realize
the most beautiful parts of your life
sprout out from your brokenness &

and nothing that is
linear created any beauty

please don't try to get your old life back

it's going to make you
chase an impossible task ahead
and a lot more suffering
that comes with such a blind chase

aim for new, aim for learning
aim for being ok
in figuring out the phase you are in

it's a self-torture to aim for the same
when nothing is the same
you must learn to love the new you
yes, the new you with uncertainty
the new you with anxiety
the new you that is falling apart
because even though
the- new- that you have is
unfamiliar, and scary, and unwarranted,
and nothing that you deserve

but it is here
and it is more real,
and it is truer than
what was old
….

.... you cannot bargain with the past
you can wish for the past to return
the freedom, hopes, and dreams
the goodness that you believed in
the absence of anger & presence of love
but still,
you cannot bargain with the past
because it is dead
and you are staying in the funeral of time
thinking it is your own funeral
when it is not

so, hold my hand
i will show you the lovely parts
of broken you
i will show you art in colors
that your soul created when
you fell apart
i will show you the music
in your tears
i will show you strength
in your bruises
and bravery in stories
you lived through

you are in a long-term relationship with yourself
in good times and in bad times....

.... you have it in you
to write new stories
in the middle of deaths and diseases
in the middle of rage and injustice

hold my hand and i will tell you
how to be ok
with the lack of peace
and i will tell you
how not everything needs to be ok
how not everything needs to be right
how not everything needs to be aligned
how not everything needs to be balanced
in sync, or comfortable
to claim and live your own life

so yes, feel wronged, feel raged
feel anxious, feel the pain
but feel the love amidst all of this
for a soul that is still alive
and breathing in you

learn to love yourself
in good times and in bad times
in pretty and ugly, in darkness and light
in sickness and health, in the known and unknown....

….and that my dear is
the kind of love that
will set you free
and liberate you from
limits you have
imprisoned yourself in

don't try to go back to the old you
the new you need you
more than ever
the death of old you
is the birth of new you

and i want you to know
no matter how shrill
the labor pains of new you - are-
it's the most beautiful
and inevitable part of your living here

the funeral is over, come let's go

set shame on fire, to set self free

your goal is not a pot of gold
at the end of the rainbow,
but doing necessary, at times boring, hard things,
with a structure and discipline at times
without a rainbow in the sight –
amidst the storm, rainy days, grey skies,
a lot of bruises, a lot of disappointments
from who you are, to who you are becoming

so today if you are not who you want to be
so today if you are not where you want to be
what matters is, which direction
you have directed all of you at
and if you did not make an inch of progress
because or despite anything or anyone
you give yourself another day
to get up and move forward
your movement decides the moment
that will take you closer to –where you want to be
and who you want to be

you rest, you recover, you repent, you regret, and
you reset and retake yourself – forward
till you have this moment, you have the power
what do you want to do with your power today

we all are swimming in the ocean of suffering
with few islands of joys
your tragedy is not an exception,
but a rule of life
and so is your joy

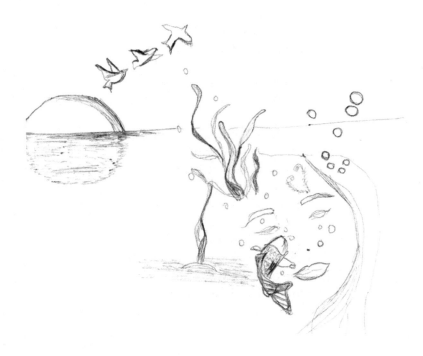

it will never be all okay

it may seem like that for some time
but the universe creates itself through your unrest
that's where newness is born
you will have new challenges
that you will not know what to do with
you will have your old challenges
that you still will not know what to do with,

amidst all that
learn to be proud of the gift
that life is and that today being
alive is enough
and having this opportunity
called life is enough

we are here for the experience,
not for a win
if you wait to be happy,
you will stay more in waiting
and less in living

so, my dear just know
no matter what, today you are amazing
and even if tomorrow is not perfect
you will still be amazing

you are <u>not</u> suffering alone

not submitting to life
amidst loss and trauma
not accepting that
few losses will break you
before they make you
not surrendering
that you may never conquer
your limitations
and strengthen your strengths
that is a dead person's wish

if you are alive
pain is alive
and you will never be safe
there is no alternative
to the path that life is

the smallness of our existence
and massiveness of what we endure
most often
we cannot make sense of it
because most losses are
senseless
we can grieve on senseless injustice
jagged bleeding margins of time
and suddenness of trauma
the only comfort we are left to create is
when we make it a shared experience
we shoulder each other's pain
and let each other rest, recover, and rejuvenate
else it kills you in more brutal ways
than death itself

offer help
take help

if you let the world break you or make you
you will never have the complete ownership of you
set aside who you are, not who they think you are

your story begins there

i sat next to her
she exhales

my body has become a billboard
of the opinions of them
short, ugly, tall, thin, fat, curvy
not enough
better than others, less than others
footprints of words that came and left promises
that died after a few days of magic
wants in disguise of love, lust in disguise of adulation

men breaking doors with the promise of salvation
and looting in haste and leaving the ruins
where they came with the promise of home
but making me a refugee in my own flesh
they take- ounce by ounce-, bit by bit of me,
making me a foreigner in my own kingdom

i eat the nibbles of validation,
starving off the truth
i choke on the lies and helplessness
i stay still because my movement
may cause hurricanes
my truth may cause the storm
so, they cut me into palatable poems and songs
and put them in colorful jars
neatly decorated and pleasantly dressed
less threatening, easier on the eyes and ears
easier on the mouth
pretty and convenient,
not a lot of work ...

....

where do you put layers of time
gifted by the universe to you over the years
i ask

i bury them alive, i hear them screaming
i hear them breathing,
i don't even say a final prayer,
i don't even kiss them for being mine
i bury them before they grow as tree of life

why so much cutting of you
i ask her
she speaks-
because they are not taught or told the love
above the magazine converts
they fear the truth, they fear the reality

and how about you, i ask
she says- after so much editing of me
i don't know who i am anymore

-hold my hand- let's start with you
so, we held hands and we walked on new lands
and we walked towards her, for her

all original beginnings are crude
and at times they are cruel
because they break us
and breaking is never elegant either

but you should keep going forward anyways
because the pain is universal
whether you follow your heart or truth or not
but the pain in your original path
will be unique and usually will invite bravery

so don't wish for easy, wish for courage
take comfort in being temporarily here
be excited about what all things
are forming inside out of you
they will be shapeless at the beginning
and will be marvelous at the end

they start as art in making
but in between, they will be foggy
and needing attention without clarity
that's when you marry uncertainty,
and you make peace with your chaos
to begin is your birthright
so, begin as many times as you need to
and in as many ways as you need to
and after as many ugly endings
because to begin is to live

every ending
is a beginning

the greatest lessons come
wrapped in the greatest suffering
so,
no one else would want it
and no one else will know it's worth

true self-care looks like work at times

work with a therapist, boring workouts,
hard work of reading to acquire new skills,
discipline in diet and exercise,
making regimens that are not fun
but an important part of survival,
self-care at times is a sweat equity
with intervals of indulgence in pleasure
it is having hard talks on self-improvement
and gratitude for how far you have come
it is making uncomfortable changes
along with what is comfortable
self-care is not commercial- it is personal
it is celebrating who and where you are
and striving towards who and where you want to be
it is tears of hard work and laughter of joy
it is not a craving for perfection
but striving for the progress
it is not constantly demanding happiness from life,
but being okay with the periods,
where happiness takes a backseat and
learning through the painful hardships
and struggles of life takes the front seat
it is learning how to attach and detach
from the outer and inner world.
it is coming back to your soul
and then extending help to others when they fall
it is knowing that hitting rock bottom has the beauty of experience,
while the glamour of success has nourishment of its own
it is a place where being uncomfortable and broken
is not a death sentence
but an opportunity to be born in a newness

that, my love is self-care

you are where you need to be
to become who you need to become

you are not meeting people
you are not meeting them as an isolated raindrop
or first spring from the glacier
but a river that has gone over the lands
at times of not their choosing
at times through lovely prairies,
carrying the fragrances of rare herbs
at times burnt villages and at times thriving cities,
at times a lost dream and at times cheers of victories

so, you are not meeting people
you are meeting a moving river of experiences
that may taste sour just because of the land it visited
before meeting you without the
wisdom of cleansing forgiveness
and at times as sweet because it self-purified
like the first day of its origin from the glaciers
because it has learned to distill itself via forgiving and forgetting

so, remember you are not meeting people
and they are not meeting a person
and remember you do not have to become
a massive dumping ground of your past experiences
with forgiving and forgetting you can return
unwanted unreturned gifts of your past
and make space for beauty that you were born with and born for

towards the end, it's the same destination for all
it's time before that end, which you own- make it lovely

be kind
be very kind
to your feelings
to your anger
to your fall as a human
to your bleeding edges
to your edges that bleed others
to your lack of capacity
to their feelings
to their anger
to their fall as human
to their edges that bled you
to their lack of capacity

because
only through kindness
you can dissolve the heavy burden of all of it
as limitations of the flesh, not lack of divinity
and you can move forward
from the next moment to another
from the next movement to another
and you move lightly, softly, bravely, intently,
and most importantly kindly

so
be kind
be very kind
it will save your softness
and your softness not only saves your soul
but souls of others too
and softness is crucial
so, life can print itself on you
and you can print yourself on life

make each morning
an act of rebellion

someday when you falter because you will
remember that day does not define you
what you do in the following days
will define you

so, forgive yourself for you are human
and then radiate with all that you have
because you are divine

the prison of land can't trap
a mind that thinks freely
the spirit that lives vigorously
and dreams that breathe stubbornly

your mind is not at the mercy of the material world
your mind is at the mercy of the material world-
it's all on you

you decide and you control

to any soul out there who needs to hear this

you belong here
you are needed here
you are in this world for a reason
keep breathing till that reason finds you

at times you will lose yourself
at times you will find yourself
at times you will fill yourself
at times you will empty yourself

and during all this
you will create a unique footprint
on the curve of time
and that's why you are here

through everything that you did
through everything you became

-the universe shifted-

and so, this moment may feel lonely
but the next moment
will be brimming with fullness
you are all those moments
and then some more

keep becoming, keep going

a warrior when beaten down is still a warrior
a victim settled on a throne is still a victim

it's not where you are, it's who you are

-today- maybe you think

doesn't match the road you imagined
in life, in career, in relationships
in the knowledge of self,
maybe you think the unknown is scary
unfamiliar is unnecessary
unseen is evil and new is just that new

to that, i am here to tell you
that what you imagined what you planned
are like the first few alphabets of life
and where you are what you are, with who you are
is delivering you more alphabets
because you will need them
in the next curve of life which is as unseen
as this curve once was

so, if you hold tight and if you promise
to try to love,
even if you have failed to love,
you will find ways to love
your scared self, your confused self
your bewildered self

no matter how much you don't do it well right now
you will keep at it...

...

even if you don't do it well,
you will not quit
being in a committed
relationship with yourself
and i promise your most beautiful parts
will find you in the most uncertain of times
and they will find you
if you show up with love and open arms
so, my dear
greet your "newness"
with fear or excitement
with uncertainty or plan
with bewildered soul or calm
but greet you must
and show up you must
your kingdom
lies behind the mountains of fears
and those fears will disappear
when you walk towards them

keep going

where lies your sanity,
there lies your peace

where lies your chaos, there lies your art
where lies your pain, there lies your heart
where lies your soul, there lies your love

you may not always feel you belong here,
but i promise you are needed here
you may not see beyond what is right now
but i promise there is a beyond
i promise you beginnings after endings
i promise, time flows as life flows
and i promise, life flows as time flows

even though this moment feels like a standstill
there is a moment after this one
which will carry the movement that you need
hang in there, just hang in there

i love you

all want to walk away
from the darkness
but only a few get up

be the sun

no one has the power to take away light from the sun
because it creates its own light within
so, when anything or anyone threatens your light
go inside, and set the wildfire within
that's bravery within the setback
that's where your power lies

not outside blaming what and who wronged you
but how you can right the wrong, deep inside and outside

those that wronged you, those that have helped you
those that bled you, those that have healed you

because you can
and because you are not just a lunar reflection
because your morning is not at the mercy of anyone
because your light is more massive
because your fire is more massive
than any speck of darkness that is thrown at you
that darkness burns inside of your brilliance
instead of eclipsing you

so go ahead be your own sun

pausing and not knowing
where you want to go is better than
keep going on the same path, that is not yours

there is no closure in life usually

there will be people who will understand you
there will be people who will not understand you
there will be events that will happen beyond your control
there will be events that you will be able to control
there will be pain you will inflict on people
because you have not learned
how to deal with the pain that came your way
there will be pain others will inflict on you
because they have not learned
how to deal with the pain that came their way
there will be connections that will be magical
and will stay with you for the rest of your life, no matter what
there will be connections that will be magical
and will not stay with you for the rest of your life, no matter what

all you can do is keep trying to grow & forgive yourself and others
you will persevere, falter, and you will get up
you will fall again, get up again with the truth, and good intent
because a journey towards truth and intent is the noblest of all
because expecting perfection from self and others
is an exhaustive and lonely experience

you will realize expecting and accepting progress and process
from self and others is more rewarding and somewhat achievable
and even that progress will have several setbacks and falls
slowly you will learn to show grace to yourself and others
**and you will shift from seeking closure towards living for what is
and towards what can be**

if you don't listen to the whispers of your dreams
your soul will drown in their screams

answer the calling

knowledge, wisdom, and transcendence

a waterdrop on the lotus
an insulated observant waterdrop on waxy lotus leaf
has the knowledge of itself and its surroundings
but it's unable to immerse in it
this is knowledge

the water in the puddle
that agreed to turn into the mud-
knowing it will lose what it was
in the pursuit of its purpose to create a beautiful lotus
without the need for validation and reward
this is wisdom

the water that evaporates,
to become clouds, witnessing the land and its miracles -
embracing the unknown journey
with complete surrender to the fact that everything is connected
complete surrender to the higher purpose and intelligence
this is transcendence

whatever you hold onto will stay
hope, anger, hurt, joy, vision, shame, happiness, guilt, regret
so, my love, what are you holding onto today

faith that will save us all

we must believe in good
even when we are in the middle of everything not so good

we cannot let hate to consume us, distract us
we must believe in good and love because
that's the only way forward-
not only for the saving of our souls
but also for our future generations

we must keep doing what is right –
when we are wronged left and right,
especially when we are wronged left and right
we must keep choosing love-
even when we are hated by every corner,
especially when we are only receiving hatred

no other time in our life will -love- will have greater importance
than the times we are tempted not to choose it
so be tenacious- that's the only religion
that the universe needs from you
and that needs the highest form of bravery

that's the only way forward and for those spreading hate,
we will keep sending you baskets full of love
till you get tired of hatred and see how useless it is
we will keep setting an example of why love is all we need-
in the middle of hatred,
that's the only way to end animosity by creating kinship.

from the book- i am not a princess i am a complete fairytale

learn to create
if you can create the beauty of moments,
memory, art, or experiences

then you don't depend
on the outer world
for the beauty of life

it depends on you

the grace of acceptance

you can love yourself and still let go of the old you
when that doesn't serve the purpose
- of why you are in this world

a butterfly can't hold onto its shell of a pupa
after it has knowledge of itswings, she can't crawl now
she needs to accept wings, sky, garden, flowers
she needs to celebrate new reasons and new seasons

its purpose is to reach flowers, add beauty and do its dance

you can love yourself without the condition of permanence-
you can fall in love with the change that you are-
you can become a process
that's the beginning of learning to love without attachment

it starts first with you and your love with who you are

and replacing it with

who you can be, need to be, deserve to be
you can love yourself enough
to bury the old, you and grow a new you
that's the beginning of learning to love without attachment

that's the first death that you can learn to understand and accept

learning awareness is knowledge
practicing awareness is wisdom
becoming awareness is transcendental

i won't ask you not to judge others
it's the first survival instinct, it's hard to fight
but i will ask you to create a space
to question your judgment

allow that pause, between stimulus and reaction
information and opinion, rejection, and acceptance
and allow a pause
trust me that pause
is where the entire universe
will do its thinking for you

trust me that pause
will save you, your relationships, and others
allow yourself to be more than a reaction
trust me, it will change you, your, life
and the others around you too

question yourself before you act
when the whole of you
wants to take over the whole of you

pause before you perform

your eyes only see
what your mind sees
or what your soul seeks

she arrived like art
that was stained with wars
colored with laughter
dense with forest of tears
and ached with fire of her being
she arrived like art
which few worshipped
few hated and few just passed by
she arrived like art
which few understood and few did not
which few tried to destroy
which few tried to preserve
which few tried to own
she arrived like art
that was part demon part god and part "time"
where people got lost
and some got found
she arrived like art
that existed before her and that will exist after
she arrived like art
where, as much pain stayed as much love stayed
she arrived like art
because she did not know otherwise
and she could unfold herself without threatening
knowledge, beginnings, endings, births, dimensions, and deaths
she arrived like art
because lill saucer of time could not hold the ocean that she carried
and she could pour all of herself without apology, shame, or pride
so, she arrived like art
so, she doesn't collapse in her own density
so, she arrived like art

irina

whatever you attach your worth to
will **own** you

the major chunk of behavior
is a response to
what someone has gone through
mostly trauma
and most of it is unprocessed
the evil in people is unprocessed trauma
from the past and misinformation
and a whole lot of fear and insecurity

evil is a lack of wisdom and healing
not lack of good

what is clutter to them

is colors to the soul

your dreams
are your wings
with their own breathing minds

they may or may not
take you where you desire to arrive
but they will take you to the places
you need to visit

they will take you to people
you need to meet
they will take you
forward
and upward
in this adventure
called life

if you have the courage to spread them
and bravery to let go
and acceptance to seeing where they take you

embrace your flight over the fright

let us rise like the vibrant sun
and
let us learn to rest like the soft night

most people fear what they can become

and the knowledge of how massive they can be
pushes them to reduce themselves

if only someone told them
the pain will present itself in their way
towards themselves or away from themselves
either way it is an inevitable part of life
they would have set themselves free
a long time ago and not spend themselves

in the prison of their own making

knowledge has no value
if it's fear that guides you

all we can do is to try
try one more day of life
even when all the light we ever received is gone
we try another day in figuring out
how to become our own sun
how to set a wildfire inside of us
when we are not sure
if the sky will return the bright morning to us
we try hard and make our own world
without being at the mercy of what lies outside of us

and then we share it
with those who are tired and lost
and we do that with a lot of love and gentleness

let the fire that burns you,
become an eternal light for all

the world is full of wondrous beauty
and needed pain
both have nothing to offer without each other

you have borrowed
you have birthed
you have drowned
you have surged
you have died
you have recovered
you have learned
you have unlearned
you have loved
you have shared
you have been pained
you have cared
you have conquered
you have failed
you have walked on the bleeding sun
you have been pierced by broken hums
you have been worshipped
you have been demolished
you have seen
you have been blinded
you have shattered
you have saved
you have carved what you have gained
you have repented
you have resurfaced
you have fallen on words unsaid
you have bruised on thorny ache
you have been found
you have been lost

but you kept your soul
to come back home

talk to your pain
it must be allowed to speak
to you
to your soul
you must let it speak
before it stays
before it slays
as a noise
that you don't understand
you must learn
what it has to say
give it time
give it ear
give it pause
give it you
let it empty itself of itself
else it will carry you forever
and you will carry it forever
when silence is violence

you cannot attach your worth

to just being productive
productivity is one of several outcomes
of who you are
take time to just be
it's not a race,
you deciding to be here is enough at times

allow yourself pace and space

bravery
is not the absence of fear
but choosing
to follow your path
despite your fear

as i grow older
i am realizing more and more
it's not enough to be right

it's more important
to be kinder to those
who are wrong

and looking back
it will be a saving grace
when you realize
so many times
what you felt and believed was right
indeed, was not
you were wrong

and just because
you were kinder to the person
the situation you did not agree with

you will heal easier
and you will learn easier
and you will shift

from being right to being better

you must remind yourself

that darkness of the night
does not mean the death of the sun

forgiving someone

is the most courageous thing you will do in this lifetime
loving someone
is the most important thing you will do in this lifetime
failing at something and at someone
will be the most necessary thing you will do in this lifetime
making boundaries
will be the most crucial part of survival you will do in this lifetime
churning compassion for others from your pain
will be the most relevant thing you will do in this lifetime
pursuing your true passion
towards becoming someone that you aspire to become
and helping at least one soul along that journey
will be the most authentic thing you will do in this lifetime
and doing all of that
while embracing breaking for becoming

will be the only way to do any of that in any lifetime

the end of time is not death

the end of the experience, is not knowing
the end of knowing, is not wisdom
the end of wisdom, is not pain
the end of pain, is not joy
the end of joy, is not suffering
the end of time, is not the absence of tomorrow
the end of time is an absence of you

the end of anything and anyone is
what you make it

the gap between
ending and
the beginning
is filled, fueled,
and finished by you

**the end ends or begins-
it's all on you**

do not postpone your joy

people ask me why i dress up every day,
so, these are the things i do every day
listening to my heart that i love
doing what i love, wearing what i love
talking to the people that i love
writing what i love, singing what i love
drinking what i love, eating chocolates that i love
connecting with people, that i love

working on my today as a gift to my tomorrow
making people around me joyful, that i love
making boundaries with the people who are yet to evolve
living my truth, that i love,
embracing my pain, that i love
indulging in lill pleasure as i pursue my purpose, that i love

i do not postpone my joy
i don't lock down my dresses, dreams, ambitions, conversations,
meals, or chocolates for tomorrow

because tomorrow is a beautiful promise,
but today is a breathing beauty
and i make my home in my today

**live in what all is love,
it fuels life**

memory lanes are full of flowers
because our minds pick out
the thorns it can't bear

to rub again, to rub against

so, remembering
someone and something will
be as much full of truth
as empty of truth

nostalgia is as much lies
as much it is not

you do not shorten the height of your soul

hide the iridescent colors of your dreams
and dim the sun inside your bones
because people
do not know what magic looks like,
feels like, and to be with like

don't you ever be ashamed
of being a unicorn in the cult of horses
don't you ever not spread your colorful wings
because others are still trapped in their shell
don't you ever hush the song that you are born with
just because music is foreign to them

you be you

the sun cannot pretend
to be a candle for long
it's ok to be a morning of all,
instead of the light of one

every single day you have a choice

to be kind, to be humble
to treat another human being with dignity
to be present and to listen
every single day you have a choice to follow your truth
to stand up for someone who cannot for himself or herself
to be a voice for voiceless
to live in your exactness
to be lost in your own path than be numb in someone else
every single day you have a choice to do right by someone
to uplift someone
to uplift yourself
to value virtues
to be brave

every single day brings the power of possibilities
every single day who you want to be
every single day you can rewrite, redo, rebuild, reconstruct

e v e r y   s i n g l e   d a y

till you have no more of them left

love and kindness should precede
everything,
every action, and every conversation
you are about to have

and it will always take
you in the right direction

the world is full of contradictions

they say you need to fail
but cringe when you do

they say change is a necessity
but get scared when it happens,
they say growth is vital to life
but reject the process, pain, and death associated with it

they say diversity in thoughts is the cornerstone of progress
but mock, laugh, punish, and obstruct those
with different ideas and different anything

they say bravery is necessary
but live-in fear and push you to do the same

but here is the good news
the world is full of contradictions, but you don't have to be

no one knows your vision
no one can know your vision
it's the most intimate relationship
between your soul & the universe
the dreams that choose you
breathe through your vision
and realize through your actions

the world may never be ready
for what you have to offer
but that should not matter

you be ready with
what you have to offer
and the cosmos
will create space for that
and that's why you are here

the good news is that you will not have a convenient life

you will have a transformative life

pain will arrive early; learning will arrive late
amidst that is a space and life meets you there
from the book- pillow of dreams

**the difference
between courage and fear**
is that
courage allows you to fly before you fall
and then takes the brilliant opportunity
to learn how to take off from the fallen flight

but fear arrests your wings
and you never get to view the wind,
the sky, the vision, the priceless high of the purpose
the journey that was always yours
the reason for your very being

**courage infuses life into the living
fear removes that very magic**

we live, we see, we learn, we love
through and within the confines of our minds
once we learn that
we decorate, clean, restructure, refurbish and
refinish the space that matters the most
-our mind

there is not a single soul

who doesn't carry incredible gifts
to deliver to this world
every soul is born with greatness,
but it needs a lot of
passion, awareness, bravery, and work
from the vessel of flesh
to deliver its greatness
in the material world
and
manifesting that gift
is the highest form of meditation

there is nothing more transcendental
than being one with why you are here
there is nothing more transcendental
than being one with your purpose and manifesting it

you carry the gifts within- that are unique to you

the problem in making a home in someone else
is that you do not know what they are made up of
where the massive cracks are
where and how the foundation is
how strongly they have cemented themselves in storm
so, when they fall apart
you become a refugee without a shore
in the land that is the sea
give your heart but keep your courage

your crown is big, magnificent, and beautiful
and you have earned it and build it over years

you don't need to pluck the rare brilliance of gems
and cut it short for another's soul to hold it

you need someone with a bigger soul
not wish your glory to be shortened to fit
in their hands and heart

do not dim your light for no one
**don't apologize for
your majestic height and wings**

allow redemption for self and others
redemption allows rebirth that we all deserve

people who do not understand
change, growth, transformation, and transition

the birth of the day
looks to them as the death of the night
a sprouting plant
looks to them as the death of the seed
and a fluttering butterfly
looks to them as the death of the pupa

that's where your power lies
in knowing, accepting, and transforming
with power and presence of change
what may look like a complete
upheaval and destruction
to all
is a movement of time and
necessity of life cycle
to the soul and to the universe

your story does not need
to make sense to all
your courage does not need
to be convenient to all
your growth does not need
to be accommodating to all

transform without apologyyour
transformation is your birthright

we are not going to live half

we will live in fullness that life is
we are going to live in fullness of love and pain
we are going to live in fullness of joy and betrayal
we are going to live in fullness of breaking apart
we are going to live in fullness of being broken

we are going to live in the fullness
of bleeding while picking ourselves up
we are going to live in the fullness of glory
that slowly we will become
we are going to live in the fullness of light that we are
we are going to live in the fullness of all this and more

we are not going to live half
we will live in fullness that life is

pain opens the doors that joy cannot
enter and learn what it must teach
it will not leave till its job is done

pay attention to what it is trying to teach you

you won't just need to go forward

but allow yourself to go backward
you allow yourself to go side to side
you allow yourself to zigzag
you allow yourself at times not to move
but resting, thinking, pondering,
and crying after your tears have dried up

there is no delete or undo button
the processing and transforming of the soul
takes time, intention and so much more
and so many more dimensions

and that's not failing to move forward
that's an essential part of moving forward

because you were born in parts
that haven't found you yet
you were born whole to be more
and at times
you don't see those parts because
your eyes have not met you yet
at times you don't hear those parts
because your ears have not met you
at times you don't value those parts
as your wisdom has not met you yet…

…you happen in patches like
life happens in patches
you happen in many stories
like life happens in many stories

so, if you travel to your past,
it's okay
if you travel to your future,
it's okay
if you are not present in your present
it's okay

don't seek balance
don't seek validation
don't seek comparison
but seek self-acceptance
that is in many beginnings, not just one
that is in many endings, not just one

your soul is not a checkbox
it is the universe and beyond
and it is yours
own it and be it

your life does not need to fit in a book
your life does not need to fit in an idea or an event
it needs to expand in its own unique way
and contract in its own unique way

embrace your uniqueness

knowing self is a curse
not knowing self is a curse
but only one of them carries the depth of life in it

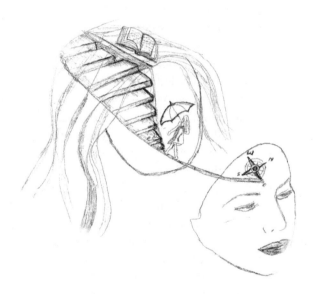

the world is a beautiful place
when we can find beauty in anything
in the fallen humanity
in the healing of humanity
in the setbacks of humanity
in the demand of justice
from the ashes of massive wrong
in the eruption of good
from the dark back of the bleeding revolution
in the screams of those silenced
in the tears of pain that shrill with fear
in the calm and comfort of justice
in the quest for equality
from the absence of love, towards the ampleness of it all
from the gaps of knowledge of what we knew
from the imperfect growing pains of what we must learn more
we must keep on with the hope and beauty
the stubbornness of that is what saves the soul of the universe
we demand what is right as we walk through
the jagged bleeding edges of the wrong
with forgiveness, kindness, and compassion
towards self and others
because we need all of us together
and we need to keep becoming our own light
as we fumble through the dark
the world is a beautiful place
when we can find beauty
in the fallen humanity, in the healing of humanity
in the setbacks of humanity, in the progress of humanity
and we keep our softness as we fiercely move forward

and when i fail to understand
i must strive to learn and
when i fail to learn
i must strive to question self
and when i fail to question self
i must be patient
till life reveals itself to me
because

we may not be where we are
we may not have arrived at who we are

but
the core belief in the goodness
of each other and self
can take us forward
amidst the path
where our jagged razor-sharp margins
can bleed one another

we must believe
that journey
will soften us eventually
will make us kinder and stronger
forgive those that hurt you
and forgive yourself
as you have hurt others…

...a heavy heart with judgment

a vision opaque with hatred
and mind convinced of only its righteousness
will not let you move forward
and to arrive where and who we are
to meet the beautiful purpose

we must unburden us
and so, we can be nimble and directed both
it doesn't have to be hard
to say i am listening
i will learn
i will keep a space for others in my heart
to send love when challenged with hatred
to send victory songs for someone else's success
when challenged with my own failure

the mind should be a beautiful place
to come home to
and there is nothing more beautiful
than a mind full of love
despite limitations of flesh

so be angry and hurt because you are human
but forgive because you are divine

there is no alternative to hope
there is no alternative to forgiveness
there is no alternative to love

a little step becomes a big step
when it is the right step
and it's the right step
when it is towards the right direction
and it's the right direction
if it's towards something good for self or and others
one day at a time, one decision at a time
life happens through one decision at a time
when we make good decisions, we are making a good life
our decisions make or break us

the villains in your story are
as tall and as powerful
as you make them

none of us are born whole

but all of us are born enough
to become and keep becoming
the reason we are not born whole is because
only that creates restlessness to be more
and in the pursuit to be more, we create,
we manifest, we grow, we learn
while seeking, wondering, yearning
moving, growing, and unlearning
and we borrow parts from each other
we borrow parts from the experiences and universe
and plants and sky and soil and friendships
and relationships and art
and literature and music and feelings

when we help each other out
with kindness and gentleness
we borrow parts of each other
instead of shaming each other
instead of punishing each other
instead of mocking each other
love flows and life flows
and that's the hug of the universe within each of us
and the one that makes us whole
it's the glue that keeps our parts together

now that we know this, we can see ourselves in each other
we can know and accept
 the pain we inflict on each other and ourselves
in that pursuit as inevitable and not the exception

we are us

you do not need to feel good
to do the good thing by you
it's another way around
when you do good by you, you feel good

you have the right to protect yourself
and say no to yourself
when you crave for- things, people, jobs, situations
that are toxic but seem safe and familiar
you have the right to stop inflicting
same suffering, same situation, the same people
who empty you, who decay you

you have the right to say no
to the addiction that self-sabotage may feel like
because it satisfies you for a few minutes
you have the right to taste discomfort and displeasure
to do right by you

you have the right to cut away parts of you
to cut away parts of your life
that will shorten your peace and growth
it's a pain that is a necessity
towards the healing that you need
towards the healing that you deserve
it's a surgery of self on self
at times without anesthesia
but still lifesaving, but still soul-saving

you have the right to protect yourself from yourself
you must use and practice that right and practice that privilege
religiously, tenaciously, and stubbornly

as if your life depends on it
because it does

when we forgive
we create extra space for love
when we forgive
we create extra space for life

i think the greatest spirituality

is to come wholesome with
vertical and horizontal growth
the vertical growth is to be one
with your mind, universe, soul,
purpose, and action
completion of that path gives
the experience of the transcendence
horizontal growth is with relationships,
visible world, material, social milestones

integrative growth is where one combines both

the greatest spirituality is to have
the roots of strength, knowledge of mortality and
impermanence, and bravery so, you are grounded
and enough chaos inside that can create and innovate
and let your soul stretch beyond who you are at a given time
as the purpose of the flesh is not to contain soul but emanate soul
to let pain teach you, to let your joy be a shared experience

the greatest spirituality is to dive into your own depth
without drowning and bring the pearls you find
on the surface, to be in service of the humanity

that to me is spirituality

at times life chooses a path for you
at times events take you where you need to be
not where you want to be
trust the journey and keep going

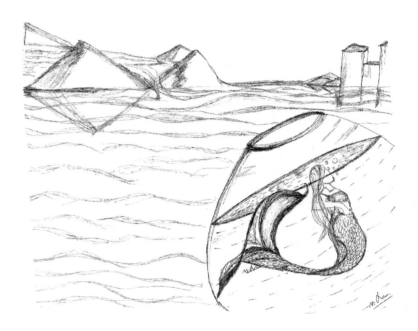

life doesn't take a pause
neither for your healing
nor for your hurting, neither for your joy
nor for your lack of it, you were not born to arrive
you were not born for a completion,
shift your mind
from completion towards movement after movement
your heart will not mend into how it was before
it will have more beauty with more pain and more art than before
pain will leave when it has taught you everything it needed to teach
joy will enter when you allow it

you cannot rush them, you can only acknowledge them
and not spend in your precious lifecurrency
in chasing and controlling, but in creating more movements
but in creating more moments
the shift from wanting to heal towards wanting to grow
where learning exist, suffering does not

choose your past as part of you
things leave, people, leave, and life leaves when it's time
you just keep traveling inside and immerse in the beauty
that comes with every experience
within laughter, within tears, within silence, within the music
it's all of you, all of it is you

and all of this is beautiful

your soul will always be taller
than the opinions of others

do what makes you come alive

be with who makes you come alive
pursue passionately what makes you come alive
anything less than that
leave, quit- take the detour, take new roads, make new roads
but do not keep walking the road that leads you nowhere
or brings you only trauma
do not, i say do not undervalue who you are
you deserve greatness- happiness
with or without something, with or without someone
don't let life pass you by,
make it move you, improve you,and shine for you
it's worth it, you are worth it

demand great things, great people, great relationships,
and above all greatness from yourself
and deliver or at least work towards not away from this
do not settle for a lesser life, participate in your own life
even if it doesn't make sense to everyone around you -
if it makes sense to you - go ahead and do it,

either it will teach you or it will liberate you

you will grow through it, i promise
you celebrate your failure
you celebrate your wins
otherwise, you will miss out on half of your life in fear or shame
set fear and shame on fire, water the garden within

you are the queen of your life,
straighten your crown and claim what is yours

there is a space
beyond your pain
it will find you, hang in there

breathe and stay

wisdom does not come
from age, time, or even experiences
it comes from being receptive
to the journey of self and others
it comes from openness- understanding -
assimilation and learning
it comes from knowing
that even knowledge has its limitations
and when those limitations we allow to
break- evolve and transform - it expands
all go through their journey in one lifetime
some run blindly, some run with map in their hand and chase the road
some run with maps in their hand,
chase the road and never lookup
some run with map in their hand, chase the road
and see the other people in their journey
and fear them if they are different
some run with map in their hand, chase the road
and see the other people in their journey
and learn from them for being different
some do not run and leave the map
but choose curiosity over fear and explore paths
and create new roads for themselves
and those coming behind them
and offer water, shade, and stories
to those in their different paths
they pause and celebrate each other
they notice flowers, stars, plants
they seek the reason for their being here on this planet
laugh lightheartedly and grow
and stay permeable to experiences then
dance through their journey

healing is not linear
grief is not linear
life is not linear

indulge in mourning
stay with aches,
greet your grief,
immerse in pain-

because the depth in life
like in art arrives
when you arrive fully

with every inch of
what life has to offer

the luscious dense flair of life
should have layers of the mist of tears
and light of joy both,

allowing yourself to be human,
even if it's harder than being divine,

but it's worth it

pain is not a burden, when it's the teacher

maybe, in the end, all you did was feel too deeply

maybe, in the end, you cared too strongly
maybe, in the end, you spend more time wondering
than discovering
maybe, in the end, you made few things,
and you broke more things
maybe, in the end, you did not get most things right
maybe, in the end, you did not find
what you were sent here to find
maybe, in the end, you did not become
what you were supposed to
maybe, in the end, nothing was what you thought it will be
maybe, in the end, the pain could not teach you much
and love hurt you more than the pain itself
maybe, in the end, what you deserved and what you got was way off
maybe, in the end, you lost more than what you found
maybe, in the end, you carried the unspoken tears beneath a heavy smile
maybe, in the end, you did or did not love enough,
but my love -
all along you lived, experienced, and went through
what you were supposed to go through
and maybe, in the end, you will realize
that life is not a balance sheet
but just a series of events
trying to let your soul expand beyond your flesh
maybe, in the end, you will realize that
the experience your soul will carry will birth new learnings
and for that, i thank you for being here
and daring through this event called life
i want you to know in the end
you paved way for something extraordinary ahead
i want you to remember that even if you don't see it
i see it and it is majestic

when we save someone else,
we are not only saving them
but we are also saving parts of us
worth saving

the contract between body, mind, and soul

the soul craves learning, the body craves desire,
and the mind negotiates with both
assigns the purpose to the soul and the pleasure to the body
all tied together with a breath.
we know parts of our physical body
here are parts of soul-energy
you can name them however you want

sun – focus, attention, self-awareness, concentration
mercury - intelligence for the material world
jupiter - wisdom and strengths, accumulated through previous births
mars - the energy of life, movement
rahu – desires, pursuit of goals and pleasures
ketu - the inner world, detachment from the outer world
saturn - the karmic justice, hardships, and delays
venus - vanity, relationships, wealth
moon - mind, from fickleness to calm,

the core of energy

shiva - destruction, endings
brahma - creation
vishnu – sustenance
krishna – knowledge that everything is transient
shakti - power, strength

....

....

during meditation - mind, body, and soul are synced together.
the same thing happens when you follow your passion
and purpose.
you already know how to take care of your body.
the way you take care of your soul is through learning and
balancing its parts/ energies.

you (the soul) have decided basic construct your life before you were born.
especially the hard times, pain, struggles, and delays- it's hard to choose
what kind of suffering you want once you are alive.

the permutation and combination of parts of the soul determines
your life's path, structure, strength, and weakness.
your strengths will allow success, survival, and joy.
your weaknesses will allow pain, failure, and learnings.

when learning is achieved in this birth, in your next birth
you gain them as your strengths.

you will keep being born till the final understanding is reached,
then you get liberated from the cycle of birth and death.
if you don't learn, the same challenges will keep appearing
in every birth.

so, staying numb or inebriated or ignoring things, or even
exiting theworld early, doesn't dissolve you of your duty
towards this learning.

....

your pain during your challenges has a lot of bearing on
your current existence but for the highest intelligence
that you are, it doesn't mean much.
but life is designed to experience every moment
with immense intensity, so growth happens,
and everything appears urgent and relevant, so learning happens

....so, death, despair and diseases do not have much meaning to the
highest form of intelligence that you are, but you experience it
intensely in your mortal form because that's how you are designed.

wishing the challenges didn't happen, trying to run away from them,
staying numb through them, or worshipping to calm your
planets through them- none of that spares you of your responsibility to
grow and learn.

once you make your pain as your teacher, you must become a
disciplined, awake, and hardworking student of it—so you can
graduate. else you keep repeating the same class of challenges in
subsequent births.

don't wish your pain away, learn your pain away.

from the upcoming book- all questions answered

forgiving, without forgetting

is not enough if you don't forget
you don't allow precious space
in your mind for something wonderful
and you don't give space for another person
to change, reform, rediscover, and regrow

forgiving frees your soul
forgetting frees your mind
and
allowing redemption for self and others
frees yourself from turning
bitter instead of better

you must believe in
the potential of being
in human beings
to be towards, to be forward
to be upwards, to be better
for those that wronged you
for those that you wronged

art is the poetry of experience
poetry is the art of experience

your voice is an important part of your existence

your voice may carry a foreign language and accent
it may appear shrill
it may have uncomfortable opinions
to those inside a box
it may not have marinated
with years of wisdom
on how to be soft and stern together

it may be threatening to those
who would rather be deaf
it may seem angry to those
who don't care about
what wrong has been done to you

it may wear colors that are too bright
it may carry fire that others can't stand
it may be so piercing
that the reality of others may fragment

it may be full of so much pain
whose weight is as foreign as lies to truth
it may carry love that no one understands....

....it may carry echoes of betrayal and
wounds that may never heal

it may be so broken that alphabets
fall behind the meaning, it wants to register

it may be content, peace, or rage of your ancestors
and ancestors before them
it may be so thick with tears and torments
that it will choke the throats of continents

it may never find an audience in this lifetime or next

it may never get applauded for being raw and real
it may look less pretty than those
who have the right color, gender, or race

it may not look like your birthright
but my dear, i am here to state
your voice is your birthright

your voice is a very important part of your existence
and no storm should make you swallow it
and let no one make you believe to be ashamed of it
it's an extension of billion-year-old stardust in you
dress it down; dress it up
but promise me you will never bury your voice
while it is still breathing, alive, and has things to say

we cannot remove our pain
we can only flower it and make it art
and make it love

sustainers and shifters

the world is changed by artists, innovators, and thinkers-
let us call them shifters
the world is sustained by sustainers and
procreators
let us call them sustainers
 while this can be a symbiotic relationship
it is often not
sustainers since often majority, outnumber shifters
and so, it's mainly their world determining awards,
rejections, validations, shames, honor, law, boundaries,
limitations, and that is the opposite of the inside world of
shifters, who are here to create unheard music,
defy norms, push boundaries, and create from the deep
womb of the universe.

but gradually they run out of the core
that fueled them and their survival is often jeopardized
because of the world created by sustainers-
they who sustain commerce, species, and a certain system,
those who have successfully clogged their pores of experiences
and focused entirely on survival of self, and society
shifters depend on sustainers for their bodily survival ...

...when sustainers finally catch up with them –
at times decades or kingdoms or centuries later –
they gratefully acknowledge how the artists or musicians
or poets or scientists or writers were so ahead of their times
and how tragic it was for them not to be supported
while they were alive

the world needs both sustainers and shifters
but without compassion and understanding,
shifters may not exist slowly

if the world becomes only about commerce –
artwork will be limited to some sketches in caves
and no discoveries would have been made

sustainers want shifters to behave like them –
to fit in a society like them - to be tame like them-
to have the same obligations and follow traditions like them –
while still inventing art, music, literature, and poetry
and innovations that are out of this world
without accepting the very core of them that rejects
all the traits required by the society of the current timeline

the people who truly create out of this world are out of this world
they are often caught between attempting to look normal
while manifesting the supernormal within them ...

….so, after fueling and attempting to be themselves
for a few years they die young, desperate, often poor

(van gogh, mozart) and were scarcely acknowledged
for their talent (emily dickinson)

 they often live a short life- but a life where
they were inside out the same- with intensity, with sensitivity,
and with a passion that sprouts from an imagination
that is more compulsive than merely existing itself

if compassion is extended towards shifters early on
sustainers and shifters can co-exist
till then shifters will just come like a shooting star
benefiting sky of their light, exhausting- and ceasing early what they have

that's why i say be kind to those around you –
who are different, who talk and create art,
who speak differently and feel differently,
those who look like they feel too much or say too much,
who have different views and are just that "different"

the world does not change by cloning but by evolving
be kind and let us learn to co-exist

**kindness and forgiveness don't need a complete understanding
but an agreement that we all need each other no matter what**

taking a step back when you need to
is an essential part of moving forward

knowing yourself starts with you

it's your job
no one else can do it for you
but you don't discover
yourself fully in isolation
you discover yourself through others,
through travel, relationships, books, experiences, events,

but none of them in isolation have any power to change you
unless you grow capacity to change
none of them can teach you about you

unless you are ready to learn
unless you humble yourself
unless your embarrassment of lack in you
is replaced by the excitement of growing something
beautiful
in that lovely land of possibility within
unless you can take pride in being under construction
instead of beginning as a completion that none of us are
unless you are permeable
unless you don't see falling in career, relationships,
vocation or whatever you give importance to ... not a
failure
but an opportunity to have an exceptional encounter with more of
yourself
unless you can laugh at your absent skills and make them learnable
skills....

....

it's not the experience, that changes people
it's people who decide to change because of experiences
from every experience, you should be able to come out of –
after grieving or after laughing or rejoicing...
you should be able to say,

this is what i learned about myself,
this is what i am considering changing,
this is how i am going to evolve
no matter who did right, or wrong

success is not the absence of failure,
happiness is not the absence of pain,
peace is not the absence of unrest,
joy is not the absence of struggle,
fulfillment is not the absence of falling
growth is not the absence of stagnation,
achievement is not the absence of scarcity,
healing is not the absence of past
victory is not the absence of defeats

life is lived in present not in absence....

.... you will be an ounce of all of this and all of that
you will never be a single story
you should never be a single story
and when you attempt to put yourself
in an airtight- razor-sharpcompartment,
of what your life should be,
the theme should be the path should be
you do not give space to let life to
expand and breathe
when you fail to practice kindness doesn't mean you are unkind,
it just means you are practicing it and there will be lapses.

when you do not arrive where you thought you will,
doesn't mean the path was less interesting,
the people you met, the learnings you learned were less relevant

when you do not get what you want doesn't mean
what you have is not worthy
allow space in your soul for stretching and breathing
andtransforming, and accepting
your biggest power lies there
you can get down from razor-sharp blade of your expectations
to lovely, calming velvet field of acceptance

....

...

and you can do your dance with life
instead of running towards the death

every virtue is to be practiced not owned
in the cracks of that practice lies the bloom of creativity
that's why being human is so innovative
your divinity gives you transcendence
but being human gives you
the ability to create through your failings and florid flaws

it's easy to be a saint but it's hard to be a person
cry when you need to, laugh when you need to
none of the emotions are less relevant
tomorrow the sun rises again, and we get another chance
to be all over again.

do not punish yourself for not being a person you were not,
when we know better, we do better.

**we can either stay in the prison of the past and penalize ourselves
or we can release ourselves from that prison to live our freedom that
arrives with- our present and future**

some losses will be your biggest gains
don't crowd your hands with regrets
make space in the palm of your life
for all the blessings you are going to create

if you are holding back
from sharing your story

you are holding back a
wounded soul to receive comfort,
that arrives from
knowing there is a community
fighting the same monster that
one feels alone fighting

sharing your story is an
elixir to the pain that is
universally isolating
untruly, unfairly, and unjustifiably
for a single person to go through
alone

your story can be the balm
for the broken wings
legs to those who can't walk
and able wings to those
whose wings are tied with
unearthly weights of shame and fear
share your words
they have
the light that
you may not see
but others seek
to end their never-ending darkness

the stories that are most difficult to tell,
are the most vital to tell

for the different women waking up differently

in the different paths of knowledge
today you get to cry your heart out justly
and let your tears wash over your heart to cleanse
what was cluttered and be okay with the stillness of pain
that doesn't make sense right now or ever

today you get to realize that you were born with the colors
that you can use to paint your rock bottom,
or you were born with the fire within
to banish the darkness that surrounds you

today you get to realize that
even making it through the last few days
have been heroic even if no one gave you
a badge of honor for that
your pride crowns your head
you are breathing till today and you did it
while falling and failing and all of that is victorious
in the context of life and living

today you get to realize that waiting
at times is part of a do-over and it is okay
today you get to grow, to absorb the possibilities
and do-little actions to take those possibilities forward
to kiss the sun, thank the sky,
appreciate your body as it carries you,
with all that you have towards becoming more,
giving more, and knowing more

today you 'get to' and not 'have to'

become who you seek

life seldom gives second chances

second chances
don't announce themselves
as the second chances
they come in the form of a new day
so today if you are alive,
that just means,
and that life
has not given up
on you yet
**and you don't have to give-up
on life either**

the thing about courage is that
you cannot demand it from others,
but you can choose it for yourself
massively, and regularly

and then soon you will choose it
stubbornly and reflexively
and then it spreads like a wildfire
you cannot demand it from others,
but through yourself-
through your courage
you can see your never-ending night
be burnt into a bright sky creating
a new day for all

courage is the foundation of all virtues
you cannot practice any virtue without courage

no one wants to hear this, but we are all addicts

we all repeat what feels good, not always what is good for us
and we all want more, its dopamine within us-
it propels the need for more, unpredictable awards
and attachment to repetitions of things that make us feel good

feeling good feels great
but when it interferes
with our survivaland purpose, it is not

media has sold moments of joy and happiness
so much that other vital nourishment
like sleep, desiring less, content,
thought minimalism, introspection, grief,
mourning, sadness
(yes, sadness is a healthy emotion), alone time

all of that - a necessary part of life
ismade to look shameful and wrong

so, find out why feeling good has become more important
than doing good
why going through hard times and doing hard things
to live and survive is looked down
an ugly crying may save you from toxic happiness

happiness is not the absence of pain,
pain is not the absence of happiness

world has a meaning that we give it
in that meaning we spend a lifetime
and next lifetime too

our death has the meaning that world gives it
you don't need to worry about that

give back, be her tribe

when you see a woman hurting and struggling, go and comfort her,
when you see a woman in self-doubt- unravel her majesty
when you see a woman setting new goals- help her out
when you see a woman breaking down- stay with her
when you see a woman falling apart- hold her tight
when you see a woman struggling with truth- be her courage
remind her that her truth is her crown- and she is only responsible for
stating her truth, not the response of others to her truth
when you see a woman doing wrong- be a friend and gently show the
way, while removing guilt that often comes with such mishaps
when you see a woman being wronged- be a goddess and become her
armor and army
when you see a woman victorious- celebrate her success and be inspired
when you see a woman confessing- value her trust and affirm her belief
that there are people who will never betray her
because when such a tribe is formed- it sets off a chain reaction to an
unstoppable force that lies within us and it is long overdue

be her tribe,
it's time for us to become that exponential power
that we are

you will never be ready for your losses
unless you see them as learning
if you can find purpose in your pain,
you will find
the lesson in your losses

balance- fact or fiction

i am usually asked how do i balance it all...
the answer is, i don't
i don't balance it all and i don't have it all
i have dreams, but they don't have me
i do let my life take over my body and health at times,
i call it my mommy weight when i gain weight writing books

for each situation of my life, i allow me grace
including pain and joy
the only constant is change
the only permanent fact is everything and everyone is temporary
so, i cannot breathe unless i am authentic and true to myself and
be in a space of mind where whatever i do impacts at least one
person positively other than myself,
whether it's through books,medicine, relationships, or art.

i don't even care about leaving a legacy
i am a breathing legacy of time like every single person
i don't want to have it all
i am not a list...

one day, i played for a few minutes with someone who was playing
basketball alone, we had a blast. i did it with my heels on and so imperfectly and
so joyfully.
so that's how i treat life, like a basketball court, join someone if you can,
by celebrating, experiencing, helping, and making someone smile...

....

you don't need to know everything,
but you should try to know as much as yourself as possible.
but no knowledge is worth without love

as in lover of all things
lover of people
lover of compassion
lover of kindness
lover of being temporary
lover of growth
lover of learning
lover of forgiveness

cheers to not having it all, for being okay with not having it all.
for even being okay with wanting it all but making sure before
you want something - you are willing to spend yourself for that.

less you desire, more you have

balance and a vibrant rich life don't coexist

you are not a robot,
you are a multi-faced storm of majestic proportions,
embrace your chaos, let it live through you,
and continue creating, destroying, and rebuilding

life is born out of movements embedded in moments

love to those who are figuring out
love to those who cannot still figure out
love to those who think they have figured out
love to those who have given up
love to those who decided against giving up
life needs all those moments
you are made of all of them - wear them with pride

flaunt being a human, it's beautiful

jt is hard but still beautiful

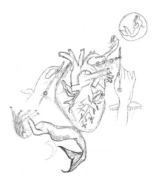

conquer within to conquer without

there is nothing more threatening
than a woman with courage

there is nothing more necessary
than a woman with courage and vision
there is nothing more relevant
than a woman with courage, vision,
and the freedom to pursue that vision
and there is nothing more powerful than
a woman with courage, vision,
the freedom to pursue that vision with a massive plan

and there is nothing more history-defining
than a woman with courage, vision,
the freedom to pursue that vision with a massive plan
and a relentless tenacity

**go ahead be any of those women
and or a woman supporting those women**

the universe cannot create art by itself

art, literature, poetry, and innovation
are born out of the limitations of flesh
the limitations that cause suffering

the denials that prolongor delay healing at
times
the passion that at times cost survival
the purpose that can cause restlessness
at risk of losing the peace

universe manifests itself through those cracks
all of that is how creation is done

the purpose for why you are here
will not show up on day one
it's a predestined series of events
that will lead you to it
you may not recognize it in this or next lifetime
but
when you are ready to receive it,
it will wake up inside of you
and when you develop skills to materialize it
it will manifest outside of you

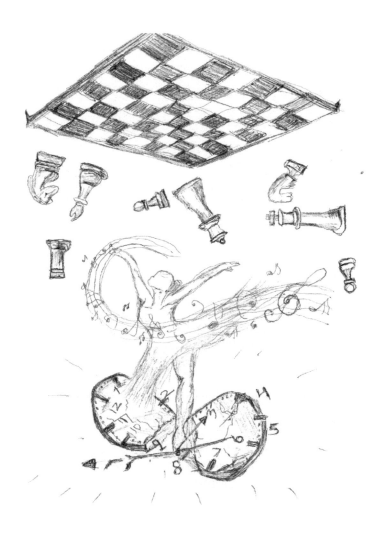

i have made peace with my chaos

i am not asking you
to forget someone or something
i am asking you
to take a step towards a new land
to take a step
towards a new anything
newness that is
waiting for you
with your name written all over
i am asking you to believe in the magic
that was always yours
that is always yours
the magic of another day
the magic of you

**healing is an outcome of
your growth**

healing is not linear
grief is not linear

there are days where victory songs come
rainbows carry all the same bright colors
and then some more
and your chest feels light enough to breathe again

till a memory walks on it
with feet carrying mountains that may not even
belong to this land
such foreign weight which no tongue has ever known to speak of
you want to go back to the days where this pain did not exist
there was no intention of it,
the joy that was as stubborn as light in the sun

but the new days
and all the days following
won't have the same hours, seconds of radiance
but a few will have absence of light
and a few will have claws of despair

and that's when you say it out loud
healing is not linear,
grief is not linear
healing is not linear,
grief is not linear

once you make peace with this fact
the jagged margins of journey don't bleed
but become friends....

.... where you can spend hours talking about
how uninteresting smooth roads are
and how much you needed
to see other paths
even those with less glitter,
rich with the absence of light at times,
shade to rest
before you begin again and again

and that's what acceptance looks like
and you sink in the comfort of knowing
that no, you don't have to make sense
of all this right now

but you do need to do
a little something good for you today
or a lot of good for you today
even when nothing feels good,
especially when nothing feels good,
and you do need to do
a little something good for someone else today
or a lot of good for someone else today
even when nothing feels good,
especially when nothing feels good

and you need to keep going
till roads get tired of your feet

**not the other way around,
not the other way around**

we must believe in the beauty that time is
we must believe that in its vastness-
there is enough space,
for the wrong that has been done to us and
the wrong, we have done to others

we must believe in its ability to carry soft healing
within the inevitable pain
we must believe in its intent
to keep giving us new opportunities

to make new decisions to wash over our past
we must believe in its fluidity
that will carry us forward no matter what

we must believe in the sacredness of its reason
to be breathing inside of our being
and keeping us against so many odds
we must believe in the excitement that it carries
which is lighter than the heavy despair that pulls us down

we must believe in its knowledge to slowly trickle down on us
bringing our wisdom to the brim, to spill over all who seek it

we must believe in the beauty that time is

pride

i was once asked what am i most proud of
and the person interviewing me was disturbed
when i couldn't come up with anything

i am not proud of anything
i don't understand that emotion

well, what made you happiest,
he insisted with curiosity

nothing makes me happy
i don't strive for it i am constantly fulfilled
with or without happiness

my thoughts flood my mind
the fragile humans going through life
covered by jagged razor-sharp margins
created by their past that bleed others
that comes close to them, are navigating through life

with an ounce of hope - doing what is expected of them
mostly what is set by the outside world and media what they
should be doing, gathering some love while inflicting pain to
self and others....

…. having minuscule time to reflect on their purpose
and intuition as they run through satisfying
what is expected of them than who they are
and still disheartened and disillusioned in a meritocratic society
that doesn't recognize any of this heroic or praiseworthy
that has set comparative emotions
that throw them more in despair than in hope or motivation

because they a shine light on few,
they honor even fewer and flaunt even fewer of them
as worthy of pride and happiness. this is exactly what is
wrong in our society.

the person who is keeping the streets clean
so, people can go to work without catching an infectious disease
the unknown rocket scientist who made crucial algorithms
the mother who accepted the permanent change
in her body and life
a lover struggling to live without someone he or she once loved
a student who is trying to constantly get back on track
fighting demons of depression
a person accepting hospice for final days in life…

....

a woman leaving a relationship that almost killed her
a woman still figuring out what to do in a similar relationship
a man hurting so bad with anxiety but trying to move ahead
with next day –

a couple celebrating their wedding anniversary
the patient with fracture finally doing well on rehab
how is all of that, less than heroic

just because the light of media is shined on very few
and few are labeled extraordinary by some people
who decided that it's their job
but that is not the truth of humanity,

truth is
as a collective consciousness,
we are trying to make sense of this temporary stay,
and trying to do it with dignity and compassion
with a lot of shortfalls every single day

being proud of myself makes me feel as if i am better than my fellow
citizens - just because some skills are more visible, and some colors
are shiny doesn't make all other colors less.

life is a process, but it's not understood by
those that shame pupa but applaud butterfly
those that shame a seed but worship a tree
those that don't find beauty in bud but only in flowers

...

if we look deep inside of us
we can value and salute the heroism of every single
person
we will not shame the seed
but applaud and appreciate its potential
we will not find a bud less relevant than a flower
because life is made up of all of this
and all of that is beautiful and needed

so, i don't carry pride
i carry the sense of urgency to learn
i carry the sense of responsibility
to soften my sharp jagged margins
created by my past

before they bleed the people that i love
because they have bled the people that i love

i carry a passion to develop skills to satisfy
the very purpose of my existence
i carry the sense of being very temporary
and in need of easy forgiveness for self and others

i carry the knowledge of being flawed and
i carry the knowledge of love and hurt
i have given to others and me, and learning
how to minimize or remove later

and none of that is pride

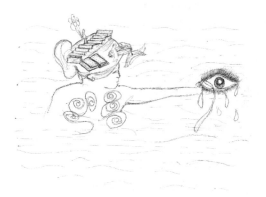

choose what and who lives in your mind
and choose that makes a garden there
and not dry it barren

making boundaries is the part of survival and healing

you are not just making boundaries against others but towards yourself.
you also need to make boundaries against your own habits, actions,
wants, and desires when they do not serve you.
when you make boundaries for self and others - you keep a home
for yourself where you can always return to - for unbecoming and
becoming within the privacy and oasis of your soul.
making boundaries is not arrogant, it is highly essential for survival.
it is to protect you, your body, mind, and soul.
you also need to make boundaries against your own desires
that take you away from your heart, mind, and soul.

make boundaries without guilt

don't be angry at the heart that hurts

that means it is still alive and loves
you would not want it any other way
you should not want it any other way

dangers of a single story

people want you to be a single story because
that's easy on the ears and eyes because they
don't have space in the library of their minds
for more than one story

people want you to have depth till their eyes can see
but not for your oceanic waves or
anything beneath it where they can drown
because not everyone knows how to
dive in your depth to claim that glorious pearl

or to live in harmony
with the city inside of you without wrecking
their limitations and without dissolving who they are

people want you to have one shade, one color,
and oneness that doesn't make them dizzy,
people want you to just declare yourself
as a hero or a villain, monster, or victim,
god or demon
and not the poetry of what it is like to be
in between or outside of what is known...

.... people want you to fit in the algorithm of
their learning because it's not their fault if they
have been conditioned to do so
or they don't have time or willingness to be otherwise

so, i will say this to you

it is ok to be a rich forest in the cities of pretty gardens
it is ok to be a lone star bursting more galaxies,
instead of being part of constellations with
their own tribe
it is ok to be pregnant with several stories
and deliver them all at once
it is ok to carry sharp edges as you learn, grow, and become

it is ok to not be understood or not to be celebrated
it is ok to be a butterfly with a grey color
or the lonely, tall tree amongst bushes of roses
it is ok to be the color that no eye has learned to see
it is ok to be a song that no one will remember in this lifetime
or next

but what is not ok is to spend a lifetime
without a day where you get to be you

find that day and then multiply it and then let it multiply you
and then lend a hand to someone, to do the same

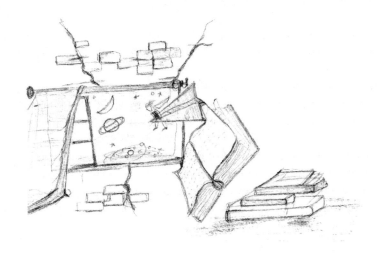

change that you resist
is the very change your soul needs

stone, sponge, and paper

arrange three small cups and add rosewater to one, milk in another, and orange juice in the last one. take a small stone in your hand - submerge it in water, then milk followed by orange juice.

when you remove the stone each time, it is left with a small film of milk, juice, and rose water and when you place it back in your palm, the stone stays intact.
now take a tissue paper and do the same. when you remove it after submerging in any of those liquids, it returns half-broken or furrowed while a small part or whole of it stays inside either of the vessels.

now take a sponge, it returns each time carrying milk- and if you squeeze it - and re-immerse it in the rose water- it absorbs that, but it never changes its essence of what it is- a sponge.

that is how people are.

the ones that cultivate a thoughtful life, self-awareness,
self-worth, courage with curiosity become the sponge,
they are soft and permeable and experience things without
losing themselves. experiences don't subtract but add to who
they are.
they will absorb experiences, relationships, travels, books, art,
and life in general, with the superpower of a cleansed self by
the way of forgiveness and making boundaries and
most importantly, still be receptive to more experiences....

…. the ones that live in fear and resist learning become stones.
they may go through trials and tribulations, relationships, life events, artistic inspirations, moments of poetry and encounters with music and other experiences but lack the courage and permeability to allow any of it to teach them something or become truly a part of them. instead, it will stay on their surfaces and quickly dissolve with forthcoming experiences.

then there are those with softness and beauty but are yet to become stronger with self-worth, self-understanding, bravery, and self-love they will become immersed in the deep way but will lose themselves completely or part of them in those experiences.

the good news is that life allows you to become a sponge, soft tissue, or a stone anytime.
we all have been each of these at different stages of our life.
the most beautiful part of it all, is that you have the power to become and unbecome.

may you recognize that power and may you become that power

some people throw away their pain
some color it and make it an art,
some ink it and make it lyrics

**some soak in it
and stay a lover, forever**

the least you can do for someone is

at times the most that they need
when you compliment a woman on her gorgeous smile,
her mind, and her dreams

when you call a friend going through deep despair
and ask her over for the tea and a walk
when you congratulate someone for their goals
when you hug someone who just lost something or someone
when you remind someone of their light amidst darkness
when you thank your colleague for doing a great job

when you say out loud- i love you- to someone
who needs to hear it the most
when you offer a shoulder to someone patiently and gently
when you recognize anger as fear and not the absence of love
when you laugh out loud with a random person who likely
needed that kinship for that day

when you say no to something or someone
and yes, to yourself for self-care
when you gift a poem to someone who is feeling alone in
their journey - or read it out loud to them

when you help someone to realize their dreams
when you remind a little girl,
she is not a princess she is a complete fairytale

the least you can do for someone
is at times the most that they need
and that's the living in life we all need

you are your repetitions,

change what you repeat
and you will become who you desire to become

**your habits are the script of your life
that you are writing**

what if we lived our life backward

from death towards life
how our outlook would be different,
how differently we will value
days, nights, life, and learning,

how quickly we will forgive
how rarely we will judge and
how deeply we will love

and how sincerely
we will be kind to each other
and how easily we will see people running
without virtues towards societal milestones
with a lot of compassion

and how truly we will care
and how easily we will welcome
joy as hope and pain as a teacher
and acceptance as peace
and curve of life as a blessing and not a surprise
and tolerance as a necessity, not charity

our ignorance stems from the fact
that mortality to each of us is just an idea
and not the truth till it happens to us....

....

it's reality and wisdom
doesn't penetrate within till
it's too late
our shortsightedness
comes from fake ranking
and greed comes from being validated as successful
to be a success in the eyes of all,
our hunger for titles and material
comes from our fear
that we won't be enough without them

what if we lived our life backward
from death towards life

how our outlook would be different
how differently we will value
days, nights, life, and learning
how quickly we will forgive
how rarely we will judge
and how deeply we will love
and how sincerely we will be kind to each other

and how easily we will see people
running without virtues
towards changing milestones
with a lot of compassion....

....and how truly we will care
and how easily we will welcome joy as hope
and pain as a teacher and acceptance as peace
and curve of life a blessing
not a surprise
and tolerance as a necessity, not charity

what if we lived our life backward
from death towards life

so, the wisdom of love
will dissolve human limitation
freeing the divine from within to without
to be one with the soul of the universe
for the collective good of all
for which we arrived here, to begin with

**what if
we lived our life backward
from death towards life**

if you open your eyes there is light
if you close them, you don't see light

it doesn't mean there is no light

same thing is true about hope
and what lies ahead of you,
just because you don't see it now
it doesn't mean, it doesn't exist

what not to say to someone who is falling

oh, you are falling
(stating the obvious)
what is wrong with you
(putting the blame)
it's over for you
(taking away hope)

instead say-
let me know when you need me
you are going to learn something
during what you are going through,

i hope to learn from you
know that i am here for you
everyone falls universally
at some point in their life-
it's not the exception but a rule and doesn't
reflect badly but bravely on you

if you are less, you can be more,
till you have the power of time and action- you got this
also isolating is a very important way
to introspect and re-prioritize....

.... society has commercialized happiness

and being together so much
that opposite of that is considered wrong
it is not, it can be very nourishing

it's like coming back home and resting
after traveling a lot-
what develops and furthers us is hard times,
that's when we grow more of us
it's beautiful and we should honor it
even if it doesn't look glamorous

your past will not be your future
if you take responsibility of your present
imagine how a good day conducive to your growth look like
and create that day in service of who you can be
and be brutally honest with yourself
it will make the pain less brutal
because - honestly of what is-
will lead to wisdom of what next
and then use everything in your power
to find, create a direction
where you will be taller than your pain

you must become taller than your pain
and it only happens when you work towards it
and towards something bigger
than who or what happened to you...

...happiness and joy are incentives
universe gives you for being here
they are not your reason for being here
but to learn and grow
learn and grow yourself
and others in that process

happiness will randomly find you
to give you hope on why you should keep living
because growth is so painful and not at all tempting
but that is precisely why we are here

life will create joy for you
lack of joy doesn't mean
something iswrong with you –
lack of happiness is not that
something is wrong with you
but hard times
are just boring and tedious
classes to graduate from
they happen so, you can be more and
indirectly the universe can be more

one day my dear,you won't be you, i won't be i

the breath be air, the sand be hair
the heart will part from this world
the victory will fail without despair
grains of us will be dispersed
& the soul will search a new haven

one day my dear you won't be you, i won't be i
the flash of time will stop for a while
to pause and kiss our minds goodbye
the love, the hurt, the victories, the splurge
the pain, the lies, the truth, and despair

the moments that could have been
the promises that should have been
the killing of dreams, the burying of themes
the truth that lied, the lie that felt right
the ache we gifted, the trauma that shifted
the empty spaces we did not fill right

the words that we should have said,
we locked inside
the passions that we killed
for convenient life

one day my dear,you won't be you, i won't be i

don't wish for someone else's life

what you see is the tip of the iceberg
there is more than what meets the eyes
your soul doesn't have what it takes
to carry the burden assigned to their soul
and their soul doesn't have what it takes
to carry the burden assigned to you

but your souls carry what it takes to help each other out
share the burden, and celebrate each other's victories
and my love you must do that
and my love you must try to do that well

joy is part of healing
do not postpone your joy

optimism should be what allows you
to know few things in life
will eventually go massively wrong
and you will have a terrible coping mechanism
but eventually, you will come out of it

optimism doesn't ask you to be happy
or hopeful, but just allows you
to imagine light at the end of the tunnel
while making sure
you know there will be a tunnel
dark dreadful of disease, deaths, disappointments
depression, and despair

it gives you a space in your mind to get ready
for such tunnel instead of creating
an illusion there will never be that tunnel

optimism should sit next to you
as you cry for days, months, or years
instead of choking you
with toxic positivity
and making you feel your reactions and emotions
are not valid and or are vicious

optimism should tell you
that gap between what you get in life and
what you deserve will most likely be
very wide and unfair
and optimism allows you to be ok with that
while you keep striving
towards being your best....

...optimism should allow you a life
with massive unjust and inequality
where you may not be able to fix anything
and at times just living through life
itself will be a great victory
optimism should remove in you
the need to be crowned a hero
to be a just owner of your own life, pride, or happiness

optimism should bring comfort
in being uncomfortable

optimism is knowing
you will have betrayals, losses,
unjust moments, and tons of darkness
and it's ok to acknowledge them
and go through them
optimism softens the suddenness of tragedy
that life is

optimism allows and accepts misery
not as an exception but as the rule of life

optimism accommodates pessimism
with grace, knowledge and meaning

optimism, is just a gentle reminder of tomorrow
after the death of 'yesterday' and at times of 'today'

you are here
neither for pleasure
nor for purpose

they just set the trajectory
of a path in your life
towards
something or someone

you are here for the growth and learning
and that knowledge will set you free from
burden of attaching yourself
to mere destination
and shift your focus
to your becoming

you must still indulge
in worldly pleasures
it gives you
nourishment of present
and transcendence
when you follow your purpose
but what gives you
freedom
is detachment from the
end results as a validation of your
being
and shift your focus to becoming

dr nivedita lakhera is a stroke survivor, divorce survivor,
heartbreak survivor and assault survivor.
she is a poet & artist by soul. she heals the body via medicine &
soul with the balm of words and art.
she was born and raised in new delhi, india. growing up in a very
loving and supportive family she walked with fairy tales on her feet.
but her otherwise beautiful life was jolted and derailed by a stroke
at the young age of 27, a divorce, and then heartbreak. she turned to
words and colors to rescue her soul. and oh yes, they did rescue her.
and now she wants to share them with everyone. she sincerely believes
beyond realms of time, classes, opinions, births, and religion that all of
us are connected by common threads of love, losses, joys, sorrows,
betrayal, support, and friendship. and so, a poem, a verse, a phrase
becomes a temple where anyone and everyone can visit and submit their
soul to rest for a little bit before embarking on the next journey, before
the next destination, before the next turn. a retreat and oasis of
belonging and familiarity... that **all hearts beat the same.**

when i am gone

i will not have eyes to see
if i left all the colors on the fingers of time
holding butterflies of my dreams
neither will i have ears
to hear the music that love is
buzzing in the souls of those
that heard my symphony of life

when i am gone
i will not have legs to run back to those
i needed to hug a lill longer

or places i should have visited but did not
or dances, i should have danced but did not
or paths i should have walked but did not

when i am gone, i will not have mouth
to say out loud 'forgive me'
to those who i have hurt
when i failed on my kindness
or say out loud 'i love you'
those i did not say enough to
or sing more songs or chatted a lill longer
or kissed a lill harder...

...or tasted sun, moon, stars
and skies a lill better
or spoken louder for those
who could not speak for themselves
or spoken softer to those
who needed that more

when i am gone
i will not have hands
to be in the service of others
to care for those who needed them
to caress my love on my skin
and on the souls of those starving of it

when i am gone
i will not have the mind
that knew (that) it did not know enough
that did not always pick the right battles
and at times drowned in anger and fear
instead of patience and courage

and at times left exquisite marvels
on the shore of life
from the pool of ancestors before me
that surprised me with joy and
ached with nostalgia...

.... when i am gone
i will carry my heart with me
as the stubborn companion of the soul
because that is where
i always lived and was accepted for the most part

that's where love began, and life began
that's where the footprints of truth stayed
and received every moment
like a sacred prayer of the universe
that was brave to love
even when it was scared to love
that wanted to keep beating
because it transcended
beyond cycle of what time is

when i am gone
i take that part of me
between the ashes
as naked bones fail to move

i will become light that i always was
without the shadow of the opaque world
and i will rise to kiss
the nothingness of unknown
leaving the weight of so much more

when i am gone

dear one,

i am leaving a few pages below blank so we can talk to each other.
more importantly so you can talk to yourself.
words after all are the nourishment of the soul.

i spent all my lifecurrency in 2020 during pandemic as a covid
frontline physician, it emptied me- and i am trying to earn it
back, slowly but surely.
to keep me accountable, i am going to use the pages below to document
my journey and i encourage you to do the same.

you can use the journal bellow to lay your pain out of your belly, to
nourish yourself with words of gratitude, motivate yourself by setting
goals and taking steps towards them.
you can share challenges, victories, emotions, love, betrayal, and
determination.
it's all for you, all of it.

thank you for being with me all through these pages.
my words are the only way for me to hug you all.
thank you for being you.

i love you all so very much.

niv

start with fear, or start with doubt
start with courage, or start without
start with hope, start with ache
start with ample, or start with scant

start with strength, or shaking hands
with bleeding back, or iron stance
start with dawn, or start with night
start with vision, or fading sight

with trembling bones or burning homes
with what is known, what is unknown
with angry roar, or softened hush
oh, my warrior, start you must

to begin is your birthright

start wherever you are- however you are

August, 2021

September, 2021

_____

_____

_____

_____

_____

_____

_____

_____

_____

_____

_____

_____

_____

_____

_____

_____

_____

_____

_____

_____

_____

October, 2021

November, 2021

December, 2021

January, 2022

February, 2022

March, 2022

April, 2022

May, 2022

June, 2022

July, 2022

August, 2022

when you feel you gave so much of you to someone

remember that person needed those parts of you
for their healing, for their path, for their life, for their becoming
for their comfort, and that is a very noble thing to do in life

we are not walking in isolation; we are walking together
we borrow some parts of each other for what lies ahead
or to heal from what was done to us and you my dear one

you have divine ability to give away some parts of you
only to grow more beautiful sum of you further
only to become softer, kinder, and stronger

the parts you gave away of you were not yours to keep
they were the reason for your being here
because in the end we all are here for each other
so please do not mourn what all you gave away
what was not yours to keep

and bask in the glory of how much more you can be
and how great it feels to fulfill why you are here

shine on

Made in the USA
Middletown, DE
17 August 2021